LIFE SYMBOLS SET

**Handbook for the 38 LIFE SYMBOL CARDS
to rebalance and heal the Solar Plexus Chakra**

Helping you to walk the Path of Processing
and let go of the mind...

Healing your life by bringing you the wisdom
to be who you truly are.

Life Symbol on the front cover: Mental Re-evaluation

Kay Kraty asserts her moral right to be identified as the author of the LIFE SYMBOLS handbooks, and to claim the LIFE SYMBOLS CARDS and concept as her intellectual property, in accordance with the Copyright, Designs and Patents Act 1988.

Text and illustrations of the LIFE SYMBOLS copyright © Kay Kraty 2009
All rights reserved.

Published by Kay Kraty

ISBN 978-0-9562042-2-6

Printed and bound in the UK by IJ graphics

Set 3 - Contents

	page
List of Life Symbols for Solar Plexus Chakra Attributes	3
The Life Symbols	4
Who they Are and What They Do	
Range of Applications	
Energetic Composition of the Life Symbols	5
Shape	
Colour	
Complementary Colour	
Number	6
Sound	
Life Symbols and the Chakras	7
The Seven Life Symbol Sets, the Chakras and What They Address	
Solar Plexus Chakra Connection, the Path of Processing	8
Chakra Colours - Key Associations	9
Colour: YELLOW	
Complementary Colour: VIOLET	
How the Life Symbols Deliver	10
Physically	
Through Visualisation	
Using the Breath	
Weaving the Aura	
Floor Work	
Using your Life Symbol Card Set	11
General Balance	
Specific Issues	
Creating a 'Story-board'	
Guidance	12
Daily Focus	
Energising Place and Space	
Making the Most of Your Life Symbol Experience	

List of Life Symbols for Solar Plexus Chakra Attributes

	page
Acceptance	13
Aloneness (All-One-ness) / Solitude	14
Analysis / Problem Solving	15
Awareness	16
Balancing Feminine Energy	17
Balancing Masculine Energy	18
Belief / Conviction	19
Change / Growth	20
Confidence / Self-assurance	21
Confusion / Indecision	22
Conscious Mind / Thought (Left Brain)	23
Cowardice	24
Discontent	25
Doubt	26
Emotional Suppression	27
Fear	28
Fickle / Moody	29
Forgiveness	30
Guilt	31
Holding on to the Past	32
Hurt	33
Intuition	34
Jealousy	35
Knowledge / Learning	36
Martyrdom	37
Mental Re-evaluation (Awakening to the new Being within)	38
Pride / Vanity / Arrogance	39
Release / Letting Go	40
Resentment	41
Resolution / Commitment	42
Responsibility	43
Self-centredness	44
Self-examination	45
Self-love	46
Self-pity (Poor Me)	47
Separateness	48
Stress / Pressure / Mental Chaos	49
Subconscious Mind / Feeling (Right Brain)	50
Glossary	51
Author's Acknowledgements	57

The Life Symbols

Who They Are and What They Do

The Life Symbols were brought into being in 2003 as a collection of 266 pictorial symbol cards, each representing a human attribute or quality which contributes to personal and spiritual growth.

All Life Symbols by-pass the conscious mind and connect directly with the subconscious. **Each Life Symbol resonates at the combined frequencies of the physical, emotional, mental, spiritual, and soul levels of being, thereby facilitating a multi-levelled rebalancing of energy.**

Using the principle of treating like with like, the Life Symbols cut quickly through long-standing blockages. Past issues are cleared without the need to re-live the pain of the original wound. The rebalancing process is completed by the delivery of an upgrade of consciousness, which is the vibratory gift carried by each Life Symbol.

Range of Applications

In addition to their use in personal and spiritual development, the Life Symbols are powerful tools to help with

- Diagnosing and treating imbalances
- Shifting long-standing blockages
- Alleviating dis-ease
- Releasing addictions and addictive behaviours
- Resolving relationship issues
- Facilitating and bringing closure to the bereavement process
- Confronting and 'working through' fears and phobias
- Healing past (life) emotional traumas

To maintain energetic integrity, each Life Symbol has been dedicated to the Highest Light and placed in its own individual 'Light-bubble'. Every interaction with the Life Symbols causes this Light to increase, which purifies their energies.

Consequently the Life Symbol Cards never need cleansing, as the continuous in-flow of Light protects their energies at all times.

Energetic Composition of the Life Symbols

<u>The Life Symbols are primarily powered by</u>

SHAPE

The shape of each Life Symbol triggers a resonance at both cellular and molecular memory level, causing a mental and/or emotional shift. To help make sense of the experience, each Life Symbol comes with an explanation of its meaning, and the gift it provides. **The gift always refers to Life Symbols within the same set, so that they can be used to complete any rebalancing process.**

COLOUR

The impact of colour is picked up through eyes and skin, literally 'colouring' our thoughts and feelings, and resonating with whatever major energy centre is attuned to that same vibration. The degree to which we find a particular colour either attractive or repellent, indicates a possible imbalance within the corresponding chakra that we may need to look at.

The colour information for each Life Symbol lists *all* the names of the symbols which belong to that particular colour 'family'. From those names, spanning all seven Life Symbol Sets, we can build up a wider picture of the attributes we might also consider, so as to ensure an equal rebalancing across all energy levels.

<u>Additional layers of information are delivered by</u>

COMPLEMENTARY COLOUR

Each visible colour is balanced by its complementary colour, the 'hidden' counterpart which offers a sub-text to the vibratory information supplied by what can be seen. Complementary colours always link to a higher frequency than that of the originating vibration, thereby providing a higher perspective of whatever is being looked at.

Again, the complementary colour information lists all the attributes which resonate with that particular vibration, extending across the complete range of all seven Life Symbol Sets.

NUMBER

Each Life Symbol has its own number through which it connects to the collective energy of all 266 Life Symbols, hence the non-sequential numbering of the Life Symbols within each Set.

Numbers are themselves symbols of universal energies, clarifying the different stages of the spiritual journey, and revealing the energetic patterns on which our development is founded.

The number on the back of each Life Symbol Card puts us in touch with the esoteric information held by its numerology, providing data which is unique in its depth and spiritual wisdom.

SOUND

Sound is a potent tool of manifestation, and one we are not always aware of. The human voice is tuned to the vibratory requirements of the body it lives in. The sounds we make and the words we use, conspire to set up a sympathetic resonance in the physical body and in the surrounding subtle energy fields. If these sounds are triggered by negativity they will manifest the same response, if not immediately then later on in the time-line. It is therefore vital to examine the feeling *behind* the sound, as that is the start-point for what we create for ourselves.

In order to shift out of old associations related to specific words, we need to set an intention which is geared to a positive possibility. Positive intent alters the way the breath activates the vocal chords, bringing a subtle potency to the resulting sound, which is heard as 'more confident'.

Many of the Life Symbols carry more than one name to give a sense of their expanded capabilities. Whatever their name or names, it is important to 'stretch' whatever meaning you ascribe to the words on the back of the symbol card.

To help this process, and to facilitate vocal experimentation, the names have been broken down into syllable-like 'sound-bites. By voicing these out loud, pronouncing them slowly and in a variety of ways, the hidden aspects of the attributes can come to the fore and be integrated within your energy fields.

Life Symbols and the Chakras

The 266 Life Symbols naturally divide into seven sets of 38 cards.

Each Life Symbol Card Set relates to the frequency of one of the seven major chakras, or energy levels, of the body, which give access to the physical, emotional, mental, spiritual and soul issues associated with that particular centre. This enables the chakras to act as pathways to all the aspects of self-knowledge and spiritual wisdom held within their vibratory range.

The Seven Life Symbol Sets, the Chakras and What They Address

Set 1   Base Chakra Connection: the Path of Experience
Issues: Recognising Spirit in matter

Set 2   Sacral Chakra Connection: the Path of Feeling
Issues: Finding the hidden self

Set 3   Solar Plexus Chakra Connection: the Path of Processing
Issues: Letting go of the mind

Set 4   Heart Chakra Connection: the Path of Exchange
Issues: Honouring the contracts

Set 5   Throat Chakra Connection: the Path of Declaration
Issues: Expressing your truth

Set 6   Brow Chakra Connection: the Path of Receptivity
Issues: Surrendering to the Divine

Set 7   Crown Chakra Connection: the Path of Mystery
Issues: Becoming the initiate

Each Life Symbol Card Set can be used on its own or as part of the whole. Sets may be used in any order, giving those who are seeking to rebalance specific issues the option to start with whichever set they feel will address their needs, without having to work their way through any previous sets.

Solar Plexus Chakra Connection, the Path of Processing

The 38 Life Symbols of Set 3 connect with the energy centre known as the Solar Plexus Chakra (literally the 'sun centre' of the body), which is sited just below the ribcage and links to the stomach, pancreas, gallbladder and liver.

The Solar Plexus Chakra handles the storage and distribution of energy to aid the digestion process, from the way the body uses food to how the mind 'digests' life. This includes the processing of all information, whether from social interactions, acquired knowledge, or from our thoughts and beliefs. As such, the Solar Plexus Chakra has a strong connection to the ego issues of the mind.

From the density of the physical body the energies gradually expand, becoming ever finer to facilitate our emotional, mental, spiritual and soul 'bodies'. At each vibratory level, we are presented with opportunities to check how far we have come in achieving balance, and what still needs to be looked at to ensure the optimum functioning of the Solar Plexus Chakra.

1. **Physical: Awareness of how we use, and are used by, power**
   Energy follows thought. Holding on to old beliefs slows down the energy so it stagnates, weighing us down and causing physical obesity. Chaotic thoughts produce stress, which blocks the power flow and causes the stomach to digest itself, resulting in stomach ulcers.

2. **Emotional: Forgiving old hurts**
   Self-pity stokes the flames of martyrdom. Honest self-examination awakens awareness of the damage we do to ourselves by holding on to past hurts, encouraging us to let go and move on.

3. **Mental: Re-evaluating what you think is important**
   Checking your belief-system and releasing what isn't yours. Giving up the need to 'know' everything. Embracing the intuitive offerings from the subconscious mind, to enhance your whole-brained thinking.

4. **Spiritual: Awakening to the balanced 'you'**
   Taking responsibility for the growth of Spiritual confidence.

5. **Soul: Accepting the holiness (the whole 'I-ness') of solitude**
   Using aloneness to access the all-One-ness of things. Expanding self-love into love for ALL.

Chakra Colours - Key Associations

As the Earth energy moves up through the body, the vibratory rate steadily increases, so that the red vibration at the Base Chakra is seen as orange at the Sacral, and yellow at the Solar Plexus Chakra.

Colour: YELLOW

Assimilation issues (vitamins and minerals, diabetes)
Communication ('Yellow Pages' directory; Mercury, messenger of gods)
Confusion
Control
Cowardice ('yellow streak' or 'yellow belly', sarcasm)
Cynicism
Digestion (ulcers, acidity, food allergies)
Fear
Gut-feel
Harvest (also: inner 'harvest' of knowledge)
Health (sunlight, vitamin C)
Intellectual pursuits and study (the need to know)
Laughter, happiness
Liver (jaundice, hepatitis)
Marigolds (associated with cleansing, healing, well-being)
Mental rigidity
Nervous complaints (skin rashes)
Scattered energy, butterfly mentality
Sun (bringer of Light, or 'en-Light-enment')
Teaching (in the Buddhist tradition yellow robes denote a teacher)
Will-power

Complementary Colour: VIOLET

Cosmic consciousness
Crises of confidence
Guilt issues
Healing
Psychosis
Sacrifice
Sensitive, prone to slights
Service
Stress
Too little thought (illusion)
Too much thought (analysis)
Transformation

How The Life Symbols Deliver

Physically

The impact of the Life Symbols is **visual** (through the eyes), **auditory** (through sounding and hearing) and **kinaesthetic** (through holding and touching, tracing their shape, or by walking or dancing their energy into the Earth). The Life Symbol Cards can be placed on the body, carried around by day and put under your pillow or mattress at night.

Through Visualisation

Bring to mind the shape and colour of your symbol of choice, step into it or see it around you to rebalance the corresponding attribute within yourself. For Planetary healing, visualise the symbol and 'place' it on, or in, the Earth or sea.

Using the Breath

On the in-breath, imagine you are taking in the symbol and/or sound of whatever attribute you want to work with. On the out-breath, let that symbol and/or sound be released through the breath, or through a whisper, and then visualise it connecting with the Light.

Weaving the Aura

Hold the Life Symbol Card a few inches away from the body with the symbol face down toward the body, then move the card in snaking figures of eight around the whole body to imprint it within the Auric field.

Floor Work

Sit, stand, or lie on the Life Symbol Cards to integrate their energies. The cards can also be placed around the room, under your chair or bed. Alternatively, lay the Life Symbol Cards on the floor in a spiral shape, creating a labyrinth which can then be walked.

Using Your Life Symbol Card Set
Some suggestions to get you started:

General Balance (all 38 Life Symbol Cards)

Lay out all 38 Life Symbol Cards symbol-side up, then divide them into three sections: those you like, dislike, and feel neutral about. Use those that are neutral and those you LIKE, to change the energy of those you DON'T, by grouping together 2, 3, or more cards, until the energy of the symbol you DISlike changes.

Next, turn over the Life Symbol Cards in their various groups, to reveal the story created by their names. Once the conscious mind has taken this in, turn the cards back again symbol-side up, for further subconscious integration. If desired, cards may be placed symbol-side against the body.

Specific Issues (specifically chosen Life Symbol Cards)

Bring a particular issue to mind, then look through the Life Symbol Cards to see which symbols 'speak' to you, or choose them by name (on the back).). For instance, confidence issues might prompt working with 'Fear', 'Confidence / Self-assurance' and 'Emotional Suppression'.

Other cards can then be added (e.g. 'Acceptance', 'Belief / Conviction' and 'Self-love') to give further insights. The symbol combinations may be looked at, placed on the body, or used in whichever way is felt to be appropriate.

Creating a 'Story-board' (all 38 Life Symbol Cards)

Lay out all 38 Life Symbol Cards symbol-side up in whatever shape you are guided to create (e.g. circle, cross, square, etc.) Be open to placing the cards at different physical levels (e.g. table-top, floor, chair-seat, etc.) with an option to hold one or more cards above the other(s).

The Story-board may contain one or more separate 'stories' which can be moved around to create a unified whole. If you have other Life Symbol Sets, these can be added to give greater insight and understanding of the bigger picture.

Guidance (5 Life Symbol Cards)

General Guidance:
With the pack of Life Symbol Cards face up: clear the mind and focus on your physical level, then cut the pack and take the card which is revealed. Do the same for your emotional, mental, spiritual and soul levels, keeping the five Life Symbol Cards in the order in which they were drawn to create an energetic profile. If necessary, additional cards may be drawn from the remaining pack to expand the information for each of your five energetic levels.

Specific Guidance:
As above, but focus on a feeling or question each time you cut the pack.

Daily Focus (1 Life Symbol Card)

Shuffle the pack of cards. Then, with the mind in neutral, cut the pack to reveal the single attribute to be kept in awareness for the day ahead.

Energising Place and Space (any number of Life Symbol Cards)

You can set the energies by placing one or more Life Symbol Cards in the environment, drawing their outline in the air or visualising their shape, in order to encourage the manifestation of their attributes in accordance with Divine Will and purpose and for the highest good for all.

Making the Most of Your Life Symbol Experience

Owing to their multi-dimensional nature, it is important to be intuitive when using the Life Symbol Cards. Therefore be guided by what you FEEL, rather than by what you think 'should' be done. When you play with the Life Symbols, they deliver their wisdom with wonderful lightness, inspiring your journey with beauty and love.

To help personalise your experience, the back of every page in this handbook has been left blank for your use, to add whatever notes or drawings you are inspired to make.

Acceptance

SHAPE   A receptacle

Meaning   Flowing with what is presented, without judgment regarding possible 'rights' or 'wrongs'.

Gift   Expanded awareness.

COLOUR   Shimmer

Acceptance; Ain Soph Aur/Source; Inter-dimensionality; Prayer; Clarity; Soul/Higher Self; Freedom; Dream-state/Illusion

Additional Layers of Information

COMPLEMENTARY COLOUR   Shell

Reconciliation; Care/Support; Beauty/Perfection; Tenderness; Adoration; Sensitivity/Gentleness; Angelic Energy; Oneness/At-One-ment

NUMBER   4

Makes things viable. Brings practical balance to situations. Relates to self-discipline and social behaviour.

SOUND   Ac-cept-an-ce

Intone to bring forth inner calm.

Aloneness (All-One-ness) / Solitude

SHAPE   Raised arms, or wings

Meaning   Being alone is often misinterpreted as being 'lonely' and viewed in a negative light, but look a little deeper and its positive message is clear.

The word 'alone' is a contraction of 'all one', and gifts us a wonderful ('one-derful', or 'full of oneness') opportunity to get in touch with the totality of being.

Gift   Soul growth.

COLOUR   Sky
Aloneness (All-One-ness)/Solitude; Willingness; Calm/Peace; Serenity; Attention/Being Present; Empathy; Patience/Tolerance; Mercy

Additional Layers of Information

COMPLEMENTARY COLOUR   Sand
Reverence/Awe (Igniting the Christ-flame within)

NUMBER   14
Expresses wisdom through words. Knows the truth of being at one with all.

SOUND   A-lone-ness (All-One-ness) / So-li-tude
Chant to encourage feeling united, within and without.

Analysis / Problem Solving

SHAPE   **Deliberate patterns**

Meaning   Builds the ability to understand by seeing all the angles. Structure and form through joined-up thinking.

The data-base created by the mind, to bring order out of chaos.

Gift   Resolving difficulties, re-evaluating ways to move on.

COLOUR   **Noon**
Analysis/Problem Solving; Conscious Mind/Thought (Left Brain)

Additional Layers of Information

COMPLEMENTARY COLOUR   **Lavender**
Focus/Mindfulness (Gathering); Humility; Consciousness; Guidance/Teaching; Forgiveness; Transformation; Healing

NUMBER   **17**
Recognises the blessing of the system we live in. Searches for perfection. Is willing to connect to the truth of what is.

SOUND   **A-na-ly-sis / Prob-lem Sol-ving**
Use vocal rhythm to bring forth a solution.

Awareness

SHAPE	**The all-seeing eye**
Meaning	Being open to, and cognisant of, all that transpires, without emotional attachments blocking the view.
Gift	Appropriate responsibility, as in 'the ability to respond'.

COLOUR   Surf
Awareness; Questioning/Asking; Integrity; Standing in Own Truth and Power; Morality/Ethics

Additional Layers of Information

COMPLEMENTARY COLOUR   Damson
Despair; Separateness; Ritual; Exclusion/Kept in the Dark

NUMBER   30
Uplifts the vision. Finds the centre of things and stays poised.

SOUND   A-ware-ness
Notice the sensory experience of speaking, and really HEAR the sounds you make. Allow what you feel to expand your wisdom.

Balancing Feminine Energy

SHAPE   **Rounded strength**

Meaning   The power of the Feminine which harbours the creative impulse, providing access to the caring aspect inherent in us all.

Gift   The ability to receive and respond to messages originating from intuition.

COLOUR   **Verdigris**
Balancing Feminine Energy; Equality/Partnership; Right Action

Additional Layers of Information

COMPLEMENTARY COLOUR   Berry
Deceit; Justice; Loneliness/Pain/Suffering; Loss/Bereavement

NUMBER   31
Makes ideas viable. Sees what is needed and enables it to happen. Births the new.

SOUND   Bal-an-cing Fe-mi-nine En-er-gy
Connect with your inner softness and speak it out into the world.

Balancing Masculine Energy

SHAPE   Strong lines, purposeful corners

Meaning   Squaring up to every-day situations.

To be effective in earthly life, we need to be sufficiently grounded so that we can keep going, no matter what.

Too much emphasis on structure promotes rigid thinking, but, when balanced by creativity, becomes the foundation for practical common sense.

Gift   Confidence to examine the self and release fear.

COLOUR   Flame
Balancing Masculine Energy; Self-centredness; Anticipation; Empowerment; Self-pity (Poor Me); Lust; Ambition/Ascension; Pride/Vanity/Arrogance

Additional Layers of Information

COMPLEMENTARY COLOUR   Verdigris
Equality/Partnership; Right Action; Balancing Feminine Energy

NUMBER   32
Has the ability to see how things work. Scientific precision. Down-to-earth communication.

SOUND   Bal-an-cing Mas-cu-line En-er-gy
Connect with your inner purposefulness, and pronounce it into being.

Belief / Conviction

SHAPE A boxed-in cross

Meaning Beliefs are useful, but their very 'solidness' limits flexibility. All beliefs start with a seed-thought, which attracts thoughts of a similar nature. Over time they become an immovable block, with the thought-mass now so entrenched that we are reluctant to change it in any way.

Mental attachments can be exchanged for new thoughts, providing we are willing to surrender what is no longer relevant (remember the tooth-fairy?) and focus on the present.

The metaphysical meaning of a cross brings together time (the horizontal bar) and matter (the vertical line), in order to experience the ever-present moment (the intersection point), which gives access to the ever-changing flow of life.

Gift Learning to let go of the past, in order to grow.

COLOUR Space
Belief/Conviction; Control; Perception; Divine Will/Co-creativity

Additional Layers of Information

COMPLEMENTARY COLOUR Rock
Judgment/Blame; Laziness/Sloth; Shame; Holding on to the Past; Frustration; Ego/Self-will

NUMBER 34
Melts down mental rigidity so that matter can be spiritualised.

SOUND Be-lief / Con-vic-tion
Speak to yourself as a Being of constant change and growth.

Change / Growth

SHAPE Coiled energy rising

Meaning Onward and upward. Venturing into new areas.

Gift Examining any suppressed emotions such as fear, resentment, or doubt; then letting them go, and accepting the situation.

COLOUR **Chartreuse**

Change/Growth; Alchemy; Journey/Process; Synchronicity

Additional Layers of Information

COMPLEMENTARY COLOUR **Fuchsia**
Sexual Energy; Greed/Excess; Karma (Action); Sacrifice/Sacrificial Love; Desire/Motivation; Gender/Sexuality; Passion

NUMBER 44
Re-evaluates the structure of matter and Spirit. Gives practical advice to facilitate the spiritual journey.

SOUND **Chan-ge / Grow-th**
Let the words expand your boundaries, to move you into the wider world.

Confidence / Self-assurance

SHAPE	**Effortless poise**

Meaning   Feeling good about ourselves and what we do. Being able to voice those feelings in a clear and calm manner.

The ability to feel confident relies on a balanced input of its two component parts, self-worth and self-esteem. Self-worth represents the degree to which we value our innate self (gender, age, height, weight, talents and characteristics), whereas self-esteem reflects our respect for what we have achieved in life (learned skills, competencies and qualifications).

Gift   Re-evaluation of old ways of thinking, commitment to growth.

COLOUR   Blaze
Confidence/ Self-assurance; Humour/Fun; Tenacity/Persistence; Positivity; Joy

Additional Layers of Information

COMPLEMENTARY COLOUR   Sea
Truth; Hearing/Listening; Speaking Own Truth; Honesty/Sincerity; Assumption; Initiation; Diplomacy/Tact; Procrastination/Postponement; Equanimity/Balance; Harmony/Unity

NUMBER   52
Explores inner feelings. Expands the heart into the mind. Holds the balance of thought and emotion, to enable truth and wisdom to come forth.

SOUND   Con-fi-den-ce / Se-lf As-su-ran-ce
Speak to confirm your worth, and assure yourself of your abilities.

Confusion / Indecision

SHAPE   **Angles of the mind**

Meaning   The 'fanatic in the attic' mentality, which heads off in all directions, unsure of the way forward.

If we spend too much time checking all the angles, we get trapped in the process, which prevents us from coming to a a decision.

Gift   Analysing the thought-process to create change.

COLOUR   **Dazzle**
Confusion/Indecision; Creativity/Creation; Resolution/Commitment;
Right Thought; Mental Re-evaluation (Awakening to the new Being within)

Additional Layers of Information

COMPLEMENTARY COLOUR   **Lilac**
Gnosis/Occult Knowledge; Mysticism/Other-worldliness; Wisdom;
Metaphysical Discipline; Spirituality/Recognising Own Divinity; Meditation;
Honouring/Respect

NUMBER   **54**
Is fearful of going beyond what has been accumulated by the mind. Holds on to perceptions of not being enough. The challenge of squaring up to inner knowing.

SOUND   **Con-fu-sion / In-de-ci-sion**
Use the voice to 'fuse' the sounds together, which can help to 'make up' your mind.

Conscious Mind / Thought
(Left Brain)

SHAPE   Operating above the surface

Meaning   The ability to record experience at will, to turn its significance over in the mind and to project forward whatever future options may be imagined, thereby 'rehearsing' the possibilities.

A clever 'information manager', capable of simultaneously sorting through old structures, while also creating new pathways.

Energy follows thought, creating scenarios which are then reacted to. As Shakespeare's *Hamlet* observes, ' For there is nothing either good or bad, but thinking makes it so.' A powerful tool, which brings into matter whatever is held in the mind.

Gift   The ability to analyse all structures and processes, in order to build up a knowledge-base.

COLOUR   Noon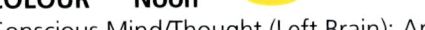
Conscious Mind/Thought (Left Brain); Analysis/Problem Solving

Additional Layers of Information

COMPLEMENTARY COLOUR   Lavender
Focus/Mindfulness (Gathering); Humility; Consciousness; Guidance/Teaching; Forgiveness; Transformation; Healing

NUMBER   56
Unconditional love, understood through the mind and managed within the self. Matter which is spiritualised, to bring about clear wisdom.

SOUND   Con-sci-ous Mi-nd / Thou-ght (Le-ft Br-ain)
Let the sounds flow, pronounce them on a single breath to bring forth oneness.

Cowardice

SHAPE   A yellow crab

Meaning   Cowering down, fearful of being noticed.

The colour yellow links to the solar plexus chakra, physically the location of the gut. Energetically this centre is associated with how we relate to the world and the degree of confidence, or 'guts', we are able to demonstrate.

If fearful of being ourselves, we end up suppressing the truth of who we are, which gives rise to feelings of anger, frustration and self-doubt. These negative feelings rip into our innards, literally 'gutting' us.

Gift   When inner discomfort reaches a critical mass, it prompts self-examination.

COLOUR   Sunset

Cowardice; Seeking/Questing; Worry; Discipline/Duty (Dharma); Choice; Completion/Fulfilment/Realisation; Silence/Glory; Courage/Encouragement; Enlightenment/Illumination/Revelation

Additional Layers of Information

COMPLEMENTARY COLOUR   Midnight

Remembrance/Memory; Subconscious Mind/Feeling (Right Brain); Intuition; Understanding; Adversity/Struggle

NUMBER   64

Squares up to service. Embraces the responsibility of being able to make things happen. Has the capacity to demonstrate 'practical' goodness.

SOUND   Co-war-dice

'Talk up' your accomplishments, be brave.

Discontent

SHAPE Out of step

Meaning Feeling short-changed, from a sense that life 'should' be better. Yet life is neither good nor bad, it just IS.

Not being content with your 'lot' may seem to depend on external issues, but is actually a reflection of how happy you are 'in your skin', and how well you accept yourself.

Gift Self-examination, the ability to look at old hurts and resentments, then let them go.

COLOUR Earth
Discontent; Stuck-ness; Blockage/Obstruction; Poverty/Lack

Additional Layers of Information

COMPLEMENTARY COLOUR Chartreuse
Alchemy; Journey/Process; Synchronicity; Change/Growth

NUMBER 77
Internalises energy and talks to the Self. Is willing to seek out and go into the central point of silence.

SOUND Dis-con-tent
Emphasise the 'con-tent' part of the word, then feel the change!

Doubt

SHAPE Checking and re-checking

Meaning Being unconvinced of the possibility of success, both in terms of what others might propose, or what we ourselves could undertake.

Gift Increasing our knowledge by committing to the experience.

COLOUR **Storm**
Doubt

Additional Layers of Information

COMPLEMENTARY COLOUR **Flame**
Self-centredness; Lust; Empowerment; Balancing Masculine Energy; Anticipation; Ambition/Ascension; Pride/Vanity/Arrogance; Self-pity (Poor Me)

NUMBER **80**
Moves away from personality issues in order to get on with the spiritual task. Accepts the job of co-creator.

SOUND **Dou-bt**
Speak lightly and with humour, to generate confidence.

Emotional Suppression

SHAPE   **Curled up in a corner**

Meaning   Keeping the lid on emotions, being frightened of letting them out.

Gift   Internal pressure and discomfort, which encourages emotional release.

COLOUR   **Wine**
Emotional Suppression; Retention; Rigid/Intolerant/Boxed In; Exhaustion; Resentment; Energy Out; Rejection/Denial; Material/Mundane/Physical; Determination

Additional Layers of Information

COMPLEMENTARY COLOUR   **Spring**
Divine Presence; Limitless Thinking

NUMBER   **84**
Brings forth practical change. Refuses to surrender to inner turmoil.

SOUND   **E-mo-tion-al Sup-press-ion**
Change SUP-pression to EX-pression. Let out your feelings and speak your truth.

Fear

SHAPE   A tomb-stone

Meaning   Fear separates, cutting us off from the unifying field of love. Through negative anticipation, we manifest what we are most frightened of, then react to what we have created, as illustrated by the acronym **F**-alse **E**-xpectation **A**-ppearing **R**-eal.

When we expect the worst, it comes into being. We create our fears and then we fear them, even though at the highest level we know that there is nothing to fear but fear itself.

The trick with fear is to look at it. This brings definition; what previously seemed an amorphous mass, shrinks and takes on a specific shape, which can then be tackled.

Gift   Fear alerts us to what we still need to work on, encouraging self-examination from a point of acceptance and self-love.

COLOUR   Coal
Fear; Negativity

Additional Layers of Information

COMPLEMENTARY COLOUR   Mist
Purification/Purity; X-ray/Cosmic Radiation; Inner Emptiness/Void; Discernment; Sacred/Holy

NUMBER   101
The rigour of spiritual work. The choice to turn away from, or step into, the Light.

SOUND   F-ear
Speak slowly and with love. Surrender all your fearful feelings to the Higher Realms. See yourself surrounded by Light.

Fickle / Moody

SHAPE	**A weather vane**
Meaning	Emotionally changeable, veering from one extreme to the other. Not sure of who to be, or when to be it. Often associated with young adults, and those with commitment issues.
Gift	Learning who we are, through what we are not.

COLOUR   **Greengage**
Fickle/Moody; Jealousy; Suspicion; Betrayal

Additional Layers of Information

COMPLEMENTARY COLOUR   Rose
Compassion; Hurt; Addiction/Habit

NUMBER   103
Detaches from the norm to gain space. Goes back to the drawing-board to check the blueprint. Chooses whether to trust what it finds.

SOUND   Fi-ckle / Moo-dy
Talk to yourself. It's ok to be 'you'.

Forgiveness

SHAPE   **Smouldering fire**

Meaning   In order to move forward, we have to let go of
old hurts. Holding on to judgments about who did what to
whom, just stirs up negative feelings and prevents wounds from
healing, which stops us achieving a neutral state.

Opening up to the new, requires that we cast off these old
feelings and offer them up, from an understanding that they
truly are 'for giving' back to the Light.

Gift   Freedom from old emotional burdens, which encourages
growth.

COLOUR   Lavender

Forgiveness; Focus/Mindfulness (Gathering); Humility; Consciousness;
Guidance/Teaching; Transformation; Healing

Additional Layers of Information

COMPLEMENTARY COLOUR   Spray

Right Speech; Imagination; Understanding the Energy of Words; Intention;
Vision/Visionary

NUMBER   105

Moves into Spirit, lets go of all constraints. Opens up to the Christ vibration.

SOUND   For-give-ness

Give up what you have held on to for so long, for your own release and relief.

Guilt

SHAPE   **Inner writhing**

Meaning   Feeling responsible for real or perceived sins, so that everything becomes our 'fault'. This creates an identity built on self-blame and leads to us become guilt 'catchers'.

Guilt 'catchers' attract guilt 'throwers'. These individuals gain power from putting guilt on others through loaded exchanges, creating guilt 'trips'. The only way out is to square up to who, or what, created that guilt, and then decide whether it is, or was, truly yours. If it is, set about neutralising its negative effects. If not, let it go.

Gift   Self-examination promotes awareness of which emotions are being held on to; take responsibility for letting them go.

COLOUR   **Glow**
Guilt; Avoidance; Self-worth; Independence; Ignorance/Bliss; Gratitude; Dependency/Co-dependency

Additional Layers of Information

COMPLEMENTARY COLOUR   **Leaf**
Trust; Vitality (Prana)/Health; Abundance/Prosperity; Altruism/Sharing; Release/Letting Go; Generosity/Giving (Gifting); Faith

NUMBER   **117**
Holds a memory of deep sensitivity, which burns through the feeling body to purify the emotions.

SOUND   **Gui-lt**
As you speak, allow the out-breath to release long-held negative feelings.

Holding on to the Past

SHAPE   Going back to the known

Meaning   Defining the present through the past. Unwilling to let go of what has long gone, either positive or negative. The perception of the 'old days' being the best, so that we avoid the 'now'.

This vibration also links to past lives. Experience imprints itself energetically, within the psyche as well as on cellular memory. Any encoding is carried forward into the next life-time, acting as a trigger to attract what is needed for further development.

Gift   Learning from old hurts.

COLOUR   Rock

Holding on to the Past; Judgment/Blame; Laziness/Sloth; Shame; Frustration; Ego/Self-will

Additional Layers of Information

COMPLEMENTARY COLOUR   Cloud
Locked in Time and Space

NUMBER   124
Moves out of the realms of Lower Nature. Begins to spiritualize matter.

SOUND   Hol-ding on to the Pa-st
Use the breath to release all vibratory 'tethers'. Breathe in the new of 'now'.

Hurt

SHAPE   The barb under the skin

Meaning   It is pointless to try and 'cover up' pain. Unless it is dealt with, its presence influences both thought and behaviour. To get rid of discomfort, we need to investigate its cause. Once the wound has been attended to, it can start to heal.

Gift   Awareness of the nature of feelings and thoughts, releasing everything that is rooted in fear.

COLOUR   Rose
Hurt; Compassion; Addiction/Habit

Additional Layers of Information

COMPLEMENTARY COLOUR   Moss
Mystery; Expectation

NUMBER   130
Presents the conflict of living in time and space. Accepts the limitations. Calls for us to stand up and be counted.

SOUND   Hu-rt
Cry it out, feel the tension being released by the body. Breathe slowly and deeply to start the healing process.

Intuition

SHAPE Energy spiralling in

Meaning Information which suddenly comes into your consciousness, causing you to 'know' without knowing how.

Although 'inner tuition' comes in at a subconscious level, the role of the conscious mind is to make sense of the messages. Therefore the better the relationship between the right and left brain hemispheres, the greater their ability to utilise the contents of these 'downloads' for our development.

Gift Knowledge derived from balanced input of masculine and feminine energy.

COLOUR **Midnight**
Intuition; Remembrance/Memory; Adversity/Struggle; Understanding; Subconscious Mind/Feeling (Right Brain)

Additional Layers of Information

COMPLEMENTARY COLOUR **Starshine**
Knowledge/Learning; Constancy/Steadfastness; Intelligence/Luminosity

NUMBER 144
Becomes a 'way-through' for inspirational communication. Teaches others from its own experience.

SOUND In-tu-i-tion
Invite your own 'knowing-ness' to come through. Trust that it will, and listen for the message.

Jealousy

SHAPE   The green-eyed monster caged within

Meaning   Not being content with who we are. Always conscious of the divide between ourselves and those we feel to be smarter or richer than we are, with better jobs or partners.

Gift   Discontent, self-pity and resentment. The resulting inner hurt can trigger self-examination and acceptance.

COLOUR   **Greengage**
Jealousy; Fickle/Moody; Suspicion; Betrayal

Additional Layers of Information

COMPLEMENTARY COLOUR   **Rose**
Compassion; Hurt; Addiction/Habit

NUMBER   **145**
Breaks down the intellect. Lets go of emotional ties. Dissolves mindsets by discovering the truth of being.

SOUND   **Jea-lou-sy**
Voice the sounds to change how you feel. You ARE enough!

Knowledge / Learning

SHAPE **Balanced brainstem**

Meaning The mental 'teamwork' required to integrate data.
Combines the logic and reason of the conscious mind, with the intuitive contributions of the subconscious mind.

Gift Confidence, the belief in your own ability.

COLOUR **Starshine**
Knowledge/Learning; Constancy/Steadfastness; Intelligence/Luminosity

Additional Layers of Information

COMPLEMENTARY COLOUR **Bishop's Purple**
Duality; Authority/Leadership; Sorrow/Remorse/Regret; Secrecy; Insight; Grief/Sadness/Trauma; Endings/Beginnings (Death)

NUMBER **152**
Yields to inner truth and wisdom. Expands into all levels of the mind. Refines information and gives out beauty.

SOUND **Know-ledge / Learn-ing**
Speak to remember that we can't NOT learn, and that we always learn more, never less!

Martyrdom

SHAPE	**A blood-stained cross**
Meaning	The agony and ecstasy of suffering. Revelling in life's wounds. Seeing hurts as a measure of the value of the journey.
	Glorying in pain, as proof of gain. Dying to what was, in order to be reborn.
Gift	Accepting responsibility for own growth. Letting go of self-pity and fear.

COLOUR**Blood**
Martyrdom; Religion (To Bind); Brotherhood/Relationship; Resistance

Additional Layers of Information

COMPLEMENTARY COLOUR**Greengage**
Fickle/Moody; Jealousy; Suspicion; Betrayal

NUMBER**163**
Expresses the vision. Purifies the perceptions of perfection. Allows the old to die, to awaken the potential of the new.

SOUND**Mar-tyr-dom**
Give voice to your pain, bring it out into the open and let it go.

Mental Re-evaluation
(Awakening to the new Being within)

SHAPE	**Breaking through barriers**
Meaning	Tearing down the restrictions of thought. Realising the joy of keeping an open mind.
	Allowing both left and right brain hemispheres to operate from a point of trust instead of fear, so we can connect with an infinite number of possibilities.
Gift	Growth through change, bringing confidence and knowledge.

COLOUR Dazzle

Mental Re-evaluation (Awakening to the new Being within); Right Thought; Creativity/Creation; Resolution/Commitment; Confusion/Indecision

Additional Layers of Information

COMPLEMENTARY COLOUR Lilac

Gnosis/Occult Knowledge; Mysticism/Other-worldliness; Metaphysical Discipline; Wisdom; Spirituality/Recognising Own Divinity; Meditation; Honouring/Respect

NUMBER 169

Crowns itself with glory and perfection. Realises the kingship of the Universal Mind.

SOUND Men-tal Re-e-val-u-a-tion (A-wa-ke-ning to the new Be-ing with-in)

Use the voice to bring in a new vibration, feel the resonance with self-love and self-worth.

Pride / Vanity / Arrogance

SHAPE **Puffery**

Meaning   Overblown energy, which is full of itself. Any bragging and showing off disconnects us from reality, resulting in the inevitably 'fall'.

However, being quietly proud of achievement reminds us of our potential to create further success. Our self-esteem level rises and we feel good about ourselves.

Gift   'Quiet' pride brings confidence, 'loud' pride reflects self-centredness, which in turn gifts the opportunity to learn to centre, or balance, the self.

COLOUR **Flame**
Pride/Vanity/Arrogance; Self-centredness; Self-pity (Poor Me); Anticipation; Lust; Empowerment; Balancing Masculine Energy; Ambition/Ascension

Additional Layers of Information

COMPLEMENTARY COLOUR **Verdigris**
Equality/Partnership; Right Action; Balancing Feminine Energy

NUMBER **191**
Gets caught up in power, and can therefore misunderstand its role. Feeds a fiery will.

SOUND **Pri-de / Va-ni-ty / Ar-ro-gan-ce**
Be proud to speak your truth and acknowledge the truth of others. We are ALL beautiful Beings.

Release / Letting Go

SHAPE	**Waving goodbye**
Meaning	Cutting the ties that bind in order to move forward. Supplanting fear with trust. Daring to set one's self free.
Gift	Change and growth, new learning and knowledge.

COLOUR   Leaf

Release/Letting Go; Generosity/Giving (Gifting); Vitality (Prana)/Health; Abundance/Prosperity; Altruism/Sharing; Faith; Trust

Additional Layers of Information

COMPLEMENTARY COLOUR   Blush

Unconditional Love; Submission/Passivity (Victim-hood); Romance/Adventure; Affection; Self-love; Childlike/Playful/Innocence (Inner Child)

NUMBER   200

Realises the need to move into a new spiral of consciousness. Trusts the process of total change.

SOUND   Re-lea-se / Let-ting Go

Allow the out-breath to set you on the path of trust. Let go and let God.

Resentment

SHAPE   **Anger pressed down, hidden grudges**

Meaning   Repressed anger taints all other emotions with bitterness and self-pity, stoking the flames of the original rage which is never far from the surface.

Gift   Internal pressure and hurt, urging a re-evaluation of events.

COLOUR   Wine
Resentment; Determination; Emotional Suppression; Energy Out; Exhaustion; Rigid/Intolerant/Boxed In; Rejection/Denial; Material/Mundane/Physical; Retention

Additional Layers of Information

COMPLEMENTARY COLOUR   Spring
Divine Presence; Limitless Thinking

NUMBER   203
Knows at a deep level what needs to be said, but is fearful of voicing its truth. Resists the responsibility of spiritual maturity.

SOUND   Re-sent-ment
Let out the hurt you've held on to for so long. Unburden yourself, set yourself free.

Resolution / Commitment

SHAPE Taking a stand, stepping up to the mark

Meaning Promising to be there come what may. Directing the energies of thought and feeling, to a cause beyond the self.

Gift Responsibility, the ability to respond to what is required.

COLOUR Dazzle

Resolution/Commitment; Creativity/Creation; Confusion/Indecision; Mental Re-evaluation (Awakening to the new Being within); Right Thought

Additional Layers of Information

COMPLEMENTARY COLOUR Lilac

Gnosis/Occult Knowledge; Mysticism/Other-worldliness; Wisdom; Metaphysical Discipline; Spirituality/Recognising Own Divinity; Meditation; Honouring/Respect

NUMBER 205

Makes up its mind to be steady. Focuses through the levels of emotion to the clarity beyond. Is aware of choice.

SOUND Re-so-lu-tion / Com-mit-ment

Make a promise, then witness yourself keeping it.

Responsibility

SHAPE   **Standing up to be counted**

Meaning   The extent to which we exercise our 'ability to respond'.

Understanding that in every exchange, our energetic contribution (however small) makes us a 'partner' in the dance of life. That, from a spiritual view, our actions and behaviours are choices which (however unconscious we are of making them), give us a degree of accountability for whatever we experience.

Gift   Being a change-maker. Accepting the concept that it takes two to tango. Forgiving, and letting go of old hurts.

COLOUR   **Ocean**
Responsibility; Femininity (Feminine Energy); Grace; Reflection

Additional Layers of Information

COMPLEMENTARY COLOUR   **Sunrise**
Self-esteem; Righteousness

NUMBER   206
Ascends to new levels of power. Manifests a pattern of right action.

SOUND   Re-spon-si-bi-li-ty
Check the quality of your response, does it come from love, or fear?

Self-centredness

SHAPE Viewing the world through the lens of 'me'

Meaning Getting caught up in the wonder of being who we are. Experiencing the very human condition of thinking the world revolves around us. Looking within to centre, or balance, ourselves.

Gift Confidence in, and knowledge of, the self.

COLOUR Flame
Self-centredness; Lust; Empowerment; Self-pity (Poor Me); Anticipation; Balancing Masculine Energy; Ambition/Ascension; Pride/Vanity/Arrogance

Additional Layers of Information

COMPLEMENTARY COLOUR Verdigris
Equality/Partnership; Right Action; Balancing Feminine Energy

NUMBER 222
Builds all aspects of selfhood, the large as well as the small. If its structure is equally weighted, it can go deeper, wider, and higher, in its quest for enlightenment.

SOUND Se-lf-cen-tred-ness
Use the sounds to connect to your core, then centre yourself.

Self-examination

SHAPE   Navel-gazing

Meaning   Diving into the Self. Mining for the gold of self-knowledge. Looking within, to work out how you 'tick'. Exploring your interior to understand who you are, and who you are not.

Gift   Knowledge of self, which helps us to learn about others. Growth.

COLOUR   Peacock
Self-examination; Connection; Recognition; Communication/Self-expression; Assertiveness

Additional Layers of Information

COMPLEMENTARY COLOUR   Glow
Avoidance; Self-worth; Independence; Guilt; Ignorance/Bliss; Gratitude; Dependency/Co-dependency

NUMBER   224
Uses the spiritual mirror to realise itself. Builds to move forward. Evolves into form, in order to survive.

SOUND   Se-lf-ex-am-i-na-tion
Allow yourself to pass your own examinations. Be kind to yourself.

Self-love

SHAPE   Allocating yourself a place in your heart

Meaning   Demonstrating approval of self. Giving yourself permission to be who you are.

When we approve of ourselves we become less dependent on external approval. Loving ourselves allows us to connect with the truth of our being.

Gift   Confidence and the ability to centre the self.

COLOUR   Blush

Self-love; Childlike/Playful/Innocence (Inner Child); Unconditional Love; Affection; Submission/Passivity (Victim-hood); Romance/Adventure

Additional Layers of Information

COMPLEMENTARY COLOUR   Sapling

Birth/Re-birth; Nurture; Integration; Hope

NUMBER   226

Expands the caring for self into caring for others. Works to serve the collective.

SOUND   Se-lf-lo-ve

Speak lovingly with warmth and affection, to acknowledge the wondrous Being you are.

Self-pity (Poor Me)

SHAPE **Waiting to be kicked**

Meaning Feeling sorry for yourself. Failing to understand that energy follows thought: that the quality of your thinking will attract like experience, as a reflection of what you have set up in your mind.

Gift Acceptance of the role you have chosen, based on what you believe to be your reality.

COLOUR **Flame**
Self-pity (Poor Me); Lust; Empowerment; Self-centeredness; Anticipation; Balancing Masculine Energy; Ambition/Ascension; Pride/Vanity/Arrogance

Additional Layers of Information

COMPLEMENTARY COLOUR **Verdigris**
Equality/Partnership; Right Action; Balancing Feminine Energy

NUMBER **227**
Brings into being what is held in the mind. Can build strong structures, as well as castles in the air.

SOUND **Se-lf-pi-ty**
Say the words cheerfully, then feel your energy change!

Separateness

SHAPE A square peg in a round hole

Meaning Feeling mismatched and out of place. Operating inside a bubble, unable to touch or be touched. Focusing on our differences, so that we feel 'at odds' with the rest of the world.

Gift Self-examination, changing the experience of feeling 'alone' to that of feeling 'all-One'.

COLOUR Damson
Separateness; Despair; Ritual; Exclusion/Kept in the Dark

Additional Layers of Information

COMPLEMENTARY COLOUR Lichen
Boredom/Indifference; Stress/Pressure/Mental Chaos; Narrow-minded/Blinkered

NUMBER 230
Tries to stay the same, struggles to stop the flow of the new. Needs to remember the natural laws of change and growth.

SOUND Se-pa-rate-ness
Let the vibrations of your words become part of the energies of the world. Love all, embrace all.

Stress / Pressure / Mental Chaos

SHAPE	**Jagged patterns**
Meaning	Mental jabs driving us on, urging us to be better and go faster. Not because we want to, but because we think we 'should'.
	The body reacts to tension as to an enemy attack, activating the 'fight-or-flight' response by flooding our system with adrenaline and cortisol, to help us do battle or run away. Once out of danger, this injection of chemicals ceases and the system returns to normal.
	However, when tension is part of every-day life, the chemical input is constant. Over time this creates a build-up of substances which damages the system, causing physical discomfort and malfunction.
Gift	Conscious analysis of what needs to change.

COLOUR **Lichen**
Stress/Pressure/Mental Chaos; Narrow-minded/Blinkered; Boredom/Indifference

Additional Layers of Information

COMPLEMENTARY COLOUR **Storm**
Doubt

NUMBER **244**
Can manipulate mind-matter. Uses inner movement to create form.

SOUND **Stre-ss / Pres-sure / Men-tal Cha-os**
Sigh out the words, release their pent-up energy. Experience the relief of letting go of the burden.

Subconscious Mind / Feeling
(Right Brain)

SHAPE   **Subterranean activity**

Meaning   That part of our mind which conveys messages by way of dreams, imagery and emotion, while also being able to tune into colour and be spatially aware.

Unlike the conscious mind, which only operates when we are 'conscious', the subconscious never stops communicating and is the prime enabler of spiritual information.

Gift   Intuitive knowledge.

COLOUR   **Midnight**
Subconscious Mind/Feeling (Right Brain); Intuition; Understanding; Remembrance/Memory; Adversity/Struggle

Additional Layers of Information

COMPLEMENTARY COLOUR   **Starshine**
Knowledge/Learning; Constancy/Steadfastness; Intelligence/Luminosity

NUMBER   **246**
The hidden rhythm which governs the human condition. The urge to trust the beat.

SOUND   **Sub-con-scious Mi-nd / Fee-ling (Ri-ght Br-ain)**
Speak the words with the intention to activate a spiritual connection. Stand by for the downloads!

Glossary

AIN SOPH AUR Kabbalistic term for one of the three aspects of the ineffable vastness that is Source. AIN SOPH AUR, or 'the limitless Void from whence all Light comes', refers to the outer eternity. Out of this beyond-ness comes the AIN SOPH, or 'that which, as yet, is un-manifest', which in turn brings forth the manifesting potential of the AIN, or 'Light'. (see also KABBALA, SOURCE and LIGHT)

AKASHA Esoteric name for the realm beyond space and time which contains all energies, confirming that there truly is 'nothing new under the sun'. (see also ESOTERIC)

AKASHIC RECORDS Energetic imprint of information on all that was, is, and ever will be, which is stored in the etheric realm. (see also ETHER)

ALCHEMY Process of transmutation. Originally associated with ancient pseudo-scientific attempts to turn base metals into gold, and the quest to create a 'magic' elixir with which to achieve eternal life. Also a metaphor for spiritual development, where the 'base metals' allude to the three lower chakras, which, when aligned with the three higher chakras, give access to the 'gold' of divine energy. (see also CHAKRA and DIVINE)

ANCIENT WISDOM Esoteric knowledge as taught in the ancient Mystery Schools to an initiated minority. (see also ESOTERIC)

ATONEMENT Old English for 'at-One-ment' or 'bringing man into harmony with God', describing the process of making amends or reparation for past imbalances.

ATROPHY Wasting process of an organ or part of the body, or the failure to grow into normal size, as a result of disease or poor nutrition.

AURA / AURIC FIELD Collective term for the subtle energy fields surrounding the dense physical body, which provide information on the state of a person's physical, emotional, mental, and spiritual balance. (see also SUBTLE ENERGY FIELDS)

CHAKRA Sanskrit for 'wheel'. A spinning vortex of energy which funnels out from the front and back of the physical body, and acts as a collector and step-down transformer of prana. Traditionally there are seven major chakras, each resonating to a frequency related to a colour which matches the vibration of a

specific area in the body. From the densest vibration to the finest, the chakras, their sites, colours and functions are as follows: Base Chakra at the coccyx, red (elimination); Sacral Chakra at the navel, orange (procreation); Solar Plexus Chakra just below the rib-cage, yellow (gut); Heart Chakra at the heart, green (pump); Throat Chakra at the throat, blue (voice); Brow Chakra at the brow, indigo (sight); Crown Chakra at the top of the head, violet (thought). Besides being barometers of organ functionality, chakras also indicate emotional, mental and spiritual balance, and act as repositories for old energetic distortions held in cellular and molecular memory. (see also SANSKRIT and PRANA)

CHRIST CONSCIOUSNESS Being conscious of the Christic Vibration. (see also CHRISTIC VIBRATION)

CHRIST-FLAME Energetic spark, or Light, inherent in each of us and connecting us to the Christic Vibration, so we can become co-creators with the Divine. (see also LIGHT and DIVINE)

CHRISTIC VIBRATION or CHRIST ENERGY Frequency which aligns with the sacred and compassionate aspects of Source. (see also SOURCE)

CONSCIOUS MIND Vehicle of the ego. Uses logic and reason to catalogue experience. Thinks in polarities, differentiates and separates. Tends to get caught up in its own cleverness and power-play. (see also LEFT BRAIN)

CONSCIOUSNESS Degree to which we are conscious of, and sensitive to, the different levels of information transmitted by the 'fire' of the soul. (see also SOUL)

COSMIC RADIATION Web of fire-light energy that permeates all things in all dimensions, all at once and eternally. Past, present and future, fused by an infinite radiance of Light. (see also LIGHT)

DHARMA Sanscrit for 'right habit' or 'duty'. The notion that all life conforms to the cosmic law of natural balance, and that everything we experience on our life-path acts as a means by which that balance can be expressed. (see also SANKRIT)

DIVINE The omniscient and omnipresent Power which governs All that Is. Eternal, spiritual and transcendent. (see also GOD / GODDESS and SOURCE)

DIVINE WILL Movement of energy instigated by the Divine, as opposed to action set in motion by human will. (see also DIVINE)

ETHER Esoteric concept pertaining to the upper regions of the atmosphere, thought to contain the blue-print of the perfection of all life-forms. (see also ESOTERIC)

ESOTERIC Obscure, and therefore beyond the comprehension of the conscious mind. (see also CONSCIOUS MIND)

FEMININE ENERGY That part of each of us, irrespective of gender, which connects to the creative aspect of the Divine Feminine principle. (see also GOD / GODDESS)

GNOSIS Esoteric spiritual knowledge as demonstrated by the Gnostics, a group of early Christians who used the superconscious to access occult information. (see also ESOTERIC, SUPERCONSCIOUS and OCCULT)

GOD / GODDESS The Supreme and Creative Energy, combining the Divine Masculine principle, or God, with its Divine Feminine counterpart, or Goddess. Also known as the Mother-Father-Creator-God. (see also DIVINE and SOURCE)

HEALING Process of bringing something or someone back to their original state of perfection. Unifying and making whole, hence 'healing' or 'whole-ing'.

HIGHER INTELLIGENCE / HIGHER MIND That aspect of the human mind which connects to the Universal Mind or Source. (see also UNIVERSAL INTELLIGENCE and SOURCE)

HIGHER SELF That aspect of our vibration which is of a higher frequency, yet inhabits the same vibratory range, which enables an exchange of energy between the 'Self', or Higher Self, and the 'self', or ego self. (see also CONSCIOUS MIND and LEFT BRAIN)

HIGHEST LIGHT The highest possible vibration and dimension we can call on.

INTUITION Knowing, without knowing how. (see also SUBCONSCIOUS MIND and RIGHT BRAIN)

KABBALA Ancient Jewish mystical tradition based on an esoteric interpretation of the Old Testament. (see also ESOTERIC)

KARMA Sanskrit for 'action'. Connects to the basic law of physics, that for every action there is an equal and opposite re-action. This 'boomerang-effect' holds true for all movements, including that of thought, intention, speech, attitude and behaviour. Once energy is activated, it increases in power, which

explains why positive outputs come back better and negative outputs come back worse. The size of the harvest is always greater than the size of the seed. (see also SANSKRIT)

LEFT BRAIN Left hemisphere of the brain which processes information through logic, reason and linear thinking. Domain of the conscious mind or ego. (see also CONSCIOUS MIND)

LIGHT Visible frequency symbolising Source. (see also SOURCE)

LOWER NATURE That part of the human energy field which resonates with the instinctive or animalistic level of being.

MANNA As in 'Manna from Heaven', which describes the process of exchange that occurs when we offer up to the Light something which we can no longer bear. Our offering is then transmuted into a positive version of itself, and gifted back to us as a blessing from the Divine. (see also LIGHT and DIVINE)

MASCULINE ENERGY That part of each of us, irrespective of gender, which resonates with the physical power and 'get-up-and-go' of the Divine Masculine principle. (see also GOD / GODDESS)

METAPHYSICAL Pertaining to the philosophical study of all things related to the Divine. (see also DIVINE)

OCCULT Latin for 'hidden'. Relating to magic, mystery, and those subtle areas which lie beyond the reasoning ability of the conscious mind. (see also CONSCIOUS MIND)

ONENESS The concept that all things in the cosmos are connected, and that every perceived 'difference' is merely an aspect of the same energy. (see also SOURCE)

PLAN Reference to Ancient Wisdom, suggesting that everything moves in accordance with the Divine Plan, to which man contributes. (see also DIVINE)

PRANA High frequency, non-physical vitality, which gives life to all living things by interacting with energy centres or chakras. Also known as Chi, Ki, Universal Life Force Energy, Holy Spirit or Holy Ghost. (see also CHAKRA)

RIGHT BRAIN Right hemisphere of the brain which houses the subconscious mind, through which we can access spatial awareness and creative imagery,

and receive intuitive down-loads. (see also INTUITION and SUBCONSCIOUS MIND)

SANSKRIT Ancient Indian language of sacred texts and philosophies.

SOUL All our yesterdays from all our lifetimes, all our energies brought to the present from the past, in order to merge back with the oneness of the Divine. (see also ONENESS and DIVINE)

SOUL SELF That part of us which mirrors our soul needs and desires. (see also SOUL)

SOURCE The originating energy out of which all is brought forth. Also referred to as Divine Energy, Mother-Father-Creator-God, Universal Mind, etc. Ultimately, that which cannot be named. (see also GOD / GODDESS)

SPIRIT Effervescent energy 'shuttle' from Source, reflecting the ever-present moment experienced. The better we are at staying in the moment, the more we can be touched by spiritual 'fire'. (see also SOURCE)

SUBCONSCIOUS MIND That part of the mind which functions below the level of our conscious ability, delivering information through dreams, images and feelings. Highly sensitive to the unaware movements of consciousness, it is a receptor for spiritual down-loads and intuitions, bringing that which is hidden to light. (see also RIGHT BRAIN and INTUITION)

SUBTLE ENERGY FIELDS The various energetic fields that constitute and surround every living thing. From the dense physical body, the energies refine in order to facilitate the subtler needs of the emotional, mental, spiritual, and soul 'bodies'. (see also SOUL)

SUPERCONSCIOUS That aspect of the Universal Mind which straddles the human 'mind-scape' and that of Source. The superconscious can only be accessed through the synergy which occurs when both brain hemispheres function as one. (see also CONSCIOUS MIND, LEFT BRAIN, SUBCONSCIOUS MIND, RIGHT BRAIN and SOURCE)

UNIVERSAL INTELLIGENCE or MIND Also known as the Divine, God, Mother-Father-Creator, and Source. The totality of all that was, is, and ever will be. (see also DIVINE, GOD / GODDESS and SOURCE)

VIOLET FLAME OF PURIFICATION Energy or Ray, also known as the Amethyst Flame, which 'burns off' all that is not balanced in order to heal. (see also HEALING)

X-RAY Electromagnetic radiation emitted by fast travelling electron particles, through which we are able to 'see into' dense matter.

Author's Acknowledgements

Many people contributed to my journey with the Life Symbols and I am grateful to them all. A special thanks to Julie Caddy for putting me on the right track and for her unwavering belief in the Life Symbols. Thanks also to Jacqui Christodoulou for her input, and to Patrick Keene for his.

I am indebted to Tim Wallace-Murphy for his on-going advice and encouragement, and for introducing me to Roslyn Chapel. I would like to thank Sarah Brown, Zuzi Griffiths and Elinor Newman for their commitment to, and participation in, the 12-month group trial, with an additional big 'thank you' to Sarah Brown who read, critiqued and edited all seven manuscripts. I am beholden to Ian Ludlow of IJ graphics for his expertise and patience.

To my family, Bryan, Robert and Felicity: my heartfelt love and thanks for their constant and unconditional support which allowed the Life Symbols to develop and become who they now are. Finally, my gratitude and thanks to the Life Symbols themselves, for coming into my life and giving me an unforgettable ride.

'Everything that happens to you is your Teacher. The secret is to sit at the feet of your life and be taught by it.

Mahatma Gandhi

Kay Kraty has a background in Eastern Philosophy and Psychology, as well as in the performing arts. A corporate trainer of many years standing, she now works as a combined energy practitioner and spiritual coach, drawing on her expertise as a voice coach, numerologist, colour therapist, crystal healer and Reiki Master Teacher.

In 2003 Kay brought through the 266 Life Symbols, pioneering this unique and multi-dimensional healing system which has, since its inception, proven to deliver powerful expansion at all levels of being.